First edition March 2021

Illustrated by Arif Setiadi
Edited by Jessica Milton

Book designed by PEN Publishing Agency
www.penpublishingagency.com

ISBN 978-1-7359166-0-6 (hardcover)
ISBN 978-1-7359166-1-3 (paperback)
ISBN 978-1-7359166-2-0 (ebook)

Published by Success Scholars LLC
www.successscholars.com

SUCCESS
SCHOLARS

THE "I AM" ALPHABET

POSITIVE AFFIRMATIONS FROM A TO Z

BY CARLOS GARCIA JR. & DR. HEATHER GARCIA

Self Affirmations

According to Merriam-Webster, self-affirmation is the act of affirming one's own worthiness and value as an individual for beneficial effect, such as increasing one's confidence or raising self-esteem. As parents, it is our job to start this process with our young children because what they think about themselves will eventually be what they believe about themselves. This is why it is so important that we teach our children from an early age to say positive statements to themselves regularly.

Helping children develop this ability is what we are hoping for with this book. With The "I AM" Alphabet, you will have the opportunity to read to your children daily and teach them self-affirming concepts that they can start to incorporate into their lives.

How to use this book

- We recommend reading this book to your children as much as possible. This not only gets them in the habit of hearing someone read them positive, truthful statements about themselves, but they have the opportunity to say the phrases out loud as well.

- One of the wonderful characteristics of our brain is that it is malleable and can be changed. When a child hears and repeats positive self-affirmations, their brain incorporates these messages, and with repeated experience children begin to assume and own the affirmative statements. We have intentionally kept the phrases short so that your child will be able to remember the words more easily. A great way for children to practice as they get older is by saying positive affirmations in front of a mirror because a mirror reflects back to you the feelings you have about yourself.

- We also want children to come up with their own self-affirmations. We have left a page at the end of the book for your children to include a picture of themselves and a space for them to write out affirmations that ring true to them. This provides the opportunity for children to practice taking ownership of the process of affirming their worthiness and value.

Dedicated to our rainbow unicorns

Gia & Bella

 I am adventurous

I am brave

Cc
I am confident

I am determined

Ee

I am energetic

I am friendly

I am genuine

I am healthy

I am innovative

I am joyful

Kk

I am kind

I am loved

I am mindful

I am nurturing

I am open-minded

I am precious

Qq

I am questioning

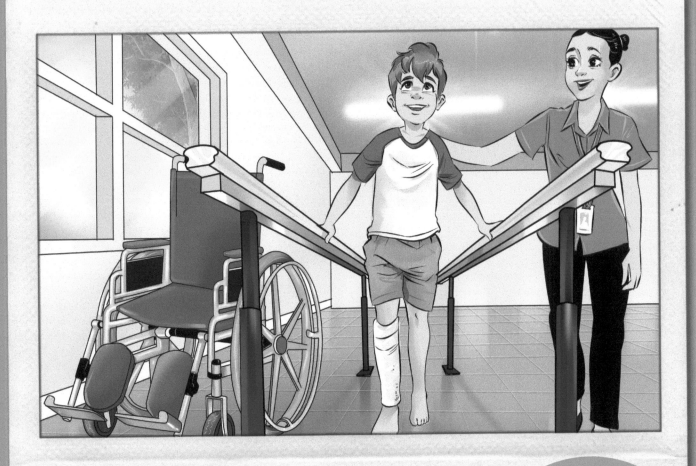

I am resilient

Ss

I am successful

I am truthful

I am unique

I am victorious

I am worthy

I am the x-factor

Yy

I am youthful